50 Rise and Dine Breakfast Recipes

By: Kelly Johnson

Table of Contents

- Avocado and Poached Egg Toast
- Lemon Poppy Seed Pancakes
- Smoked Salmon Bagels with Cream Cheese
- Breakfast Tacos with Salsa Verde
- Banana Chocolate Chip Muffins
- Spinach and Cheese Breakfast Quesadilla
- Strawberry Almond Overnight Oats
- Classic Breakfast Burrito
- Cinnamon Roll Casserole
- Vegetable and Cheddar Frittata
- Apple Cinnamon French Toast
- Bacon, Egg, and Cheese Croissants
- Sweet Potato Hash with Fried Eggs
- Banana Bread with Walnuts
- Greek Yogurt with Granola and Honey
- Scrambled Eggs with Chives and Sour Cream
- Maple Glazed Bacon Pancakes
- Huevos Rancheros
- Orange Marmalade Scones
- Ricotta Pancakes with Mixed Berries
- Chia Seed Pudding with Mango
- Mushroom and Spinach Scramble
- Coconut Flour Waffles
- Quinoa Breakfast Bowl with Almonds
- Sausage and Egg Muffins
- Apple Cranberry Oatmeal
- Mediterranean Breakfast Wrap
- Blueberry Lemon Muffins
- Savory Breakfast Strata with Bacon
- Classic Eggs Benedict
- Grilled Peach and Honey Yogurt Parfait
- Egg and Avocado Breakfast Sandwich
- Sweet Corn and Bacon Fritters
- Baked Pears with Cinnamon and Walnuts
- Sweet Potato and Sausage Casserole

- Maple-Glazed Oatmeal with Pecans
- Spicy Shakshuka
- Cinnamon Apple Pancakes
- Breakfast Salad with Poached Eggs
- Chorizo Breakfast Bowl
- Kiwi and Coconut Breakfast Pudding
- Avocado Toast with Tomato and Basil
- Almond Joy Smoothie Bowl
- Egg and Spinach Breakfast Wrap
- Chocolate Peanut Butter Overnight Oats
- Buttermilk Biscuits with Sausage Gravy
- Mango Coconut Pancakes
- Bacon and Egg Breakfast Pizza
- Yogurt Parfait with Berries and Almonds
- Grilled Cheese Breakfast Sandwich

Avocado and Poached Egg Toast

Ingredients:

- 2 slices whole-grain bread, toasted
- 1 ripe avocado, mashed
- 2 eggs, poached
- Salt and pepper, to taste
- Red pepper flakes (optional)

Instructions:

1. Spread mashed avocado on toasted bread.
2. Top with poached eggs and season with salt, pepper, and red pepper flakes.

Lemon Poppy Seed Pancakes

Ingredients:

- 1 cup all-purpose flour
- 1 tbsp poppy seeds
- 1 tbsp sugar
- 1 tsp baking powder
- 1/2 tsp baking soda
- 1/4 tsp salt
- 1 cup buttermilk
- 1 large egg
- Zest of 1 lemon
- 2 tbsp lemon juice

Instructions:

1. In a bowl, whisk together dry ingredients, then add wet ingredients and mix until smooth.
2. Cook pancakes on a hot, greased griddle until golden on both sides.

Smoked Salmon Bagels with Cream Cheese

Ingredients:

- 4 bagels, halved
- 1/2 cup cream cheese
- 8 oz smoked salmon
- 1/4 cup capers
- 1/2 red onion, thinly sliced
- Fresh dill for garnish

Instructions:

1. Spread cream cheese on bagel halves.
2. Layer with smoked salmon, capers, onion, and garnish with fresh dill.

Breakfast Tacos with Salsa Verde

Ingredients:

- 4 small soft tortillas
- 4 large eggs, scrambled
- 1/2 cup salsa verde
- 1/4 cup shredded cheese
- 1/4 cup diced avocado
- Fresh cilantro, for garnish

Instructions:

1. Heat tortillas and fill with scrambled eggs, salsa verde, cheese, and avocado.
2. Garnish with cilantro and serve.

Banana Chocolate Chip Muffins

Ingredients:

- 1 1/2 cups all-purpose flour
- 1 tsp baking soda
- 1/4 tsp salt
- 1/2 cup sugar
- 1/2 cup butter, softened
- 2 ripe bananas, mashed
- 1 large egg
- 1/2 cup chocolate chips

Instructions:

1. Preheat oven to 350°F (175°C) and grease a muffin tin.
2. Mix dry ingredients, then cream butter and sugar. Add mashed bananas and egg.
3. Fold in dry ingredients and chocolate chips. Bake for 18-20 minutes.

Spinach and Cheese Breakfast Quesadilla

Ingredients:

- 2 flour tortillas
- 1/2 cup shredded cheddar cheese
- 1/2 cup spinach, sautéed
- 2 large eggs, scrambled
- Salt and pepper, to taste
Instructions:
1. Place scrambled eggs, spinach, and cheese between tortillas.
2. Cook in a skillet over medium heat until crispy and golden, then slice into wedges.

Strawberry Almond Overnight Oats

Ingredients:

- 1/2 cup rolled oats
- 1/2 cup almond milk
- 1/4 cup diced strawberries
- 1 tbsp almond butter
- 1 tsp chia seeds
- 1 tsp honey

Instructions:

1. Mix all ingredients in a jar and refrigerate overnight.
2. Stir and serve cold, topped with extra strawberries.

Classic Breakfast Burrito

Ingredients:

- 4 large flour tortillas
- 4 large eggs, scrambled
- 1/2 cup cooked sausage or bacon (optional)
- 1/4 cup shredded cheddar cheese
- 1/4 cup salsa

Instructions:

1. Fill tortillas with scrambled eggs, sausage or bacon, cheese, and salsa.
2. Roll up and serve warm.

Cinnamon Roll Casserole

Ingredients:

- 2 cans refrigerated cinnamon rolls
- 1 cup milk
- 3 large eggs
- 1/4 cup maple syrup
- 1 tsp vanilla extract
- 1/2 tsp ground cinnamon
- 1/4 cup powdered sugar (for glaze)
- 1 tbsp milk (for glaze)

Instructions:

1. Preheat oven to 350°F (175°C) and grease a baking dish.
2. Cut cinnamon rolls into quarters and place them in the dish.
3. Whisk together milk, eggs, syrup, vanilla, and cinnamon, then pour over the cinnamon rolls.
4. Bake for 30-35 minutes. Drizzle with glaze made by mixing powdered sugar and milk.

Vegetable and Cheddar Frittata

Ingredients:

- 6 large eggs
- 1/2 cup milk
- 1/2 cup shredded cheddar cheese
- 1/2 cup diced bell peppers
- 1/4 cup diced onions
- 1/4 cup spinach, chopped
- Salt and pepper, to taste
  Instructions:
1. Preheat oven to 375°F (190°C).
2. Sauté vegetables until soft, then add beaten eggs and milk.
3. Sprinkle with cheddar cheese and bake for 15-20 minutes or until eggs are set.

Apple Cinnamon French Toast

Ingredients:

- 4 slices thick-cut bread
- 2 eggs
- 1/2 cup milk
- 1 tsp cinnamon
- 1/4 tsp nutmeg
- 1 apple, thinly sliced
- 2 tbsp butter
- Maple syrup, for serving

Instructions:

1. Whisk together eggs, milk, cinnamon, and nutmeg.
2. Dip bread slices into egg mixture and cook in buttered skillet until golden.
3. Top with apple slices and syrup before serving.

Bacon, Egg, and Cheese Croissants

Ingredients:

- 4 croissants, split in half
- 4 large eggs
- 4 slices cooked bacon
- 4 slices cheddar cheese
- Salt and pepper, to taste

Instructions:

1. Scramble eggs and season with salt and pepper.
2. Layer scrambled eggs, bacon, and cheese on the croissant halves.
3. Close the croissants and bake at 350°F (175°C) for 5-10 minutes until cheese is melted.

Sweet Potato Hash with Fried Eggs

Ingredients:

- 2 medium sweet potatoes, diced
- 1 tbsp olive oil
- 1/2 cup diced onion
- 1/2 cup bell peppers, diced
- 4 eggs
- Salt and pepper, to taste

Instructions:

1. Sauté sweet potatoes in olive oil until tender.
2. Add onions and bell peppers, cooking until soft.
3. Fry eggs and serve on top of the sweet potato hash, seasoning with salt and pepper.

Banana Bread with Walnuts

Ingredients:

- 2 ripe bananas, mashed
- 1/2 cup butter, softened
- 1 cup sugar
- 2 eggs
- 1 1/2 cups all-purpose flour
- 1 tsp baking soda
- 1/4 tsp salt
- 1/2 cup chopped walnuts

Instructions:

1. Preheat oven to 350°F (175°C).
2. Cream together butter, sugar, and eggs. Add mashed bananas.
3. Mix in dry ingredients and fold in walnuts.
4. Pour into greased loaf pan and bake for 60 minutes.

Greek Yogurt with Granola and Honey

Ingredients:

- 1 cup Greek yogurt
- 1/4 cup granola
- 1 tbsp honey

Instructions:

1. Scoop yogurt into a bowl, top with granola, and drizzle with honey.

Scrambled Eggs with Chives and Sour Cream

Ingredients:

- 4 large eggs
- 2 tbsp sour cream
- 1 tbsp chopped chives
- Salt and pepper, to taste

Instructions:

1. Whisk together eggs, sour cream, chives, salt, and pepper.
2. Scramble eggs in a non-stick skillet over low heat until fluffy.

Maple Glazed Bacon Pancakes

Ingredients:

- 1 lb bacon
- 1 cup pancake mix
- 1/2 cup milk
- 1 large egg
- 2 tbsp maple syrup
- 1 tsp vanilla extract
- 1/4 tsp salt

Instructions:

1. Cook bacon until crispy and set aside.
2. In a bowl, whisk together pancake mix, milk, egg, syrup, vanilla, and salt.
3. Pour batter onto a hot, greased griddle and cook pancakes.
4. Drizzle with maple syrup and serve with crispy bacon.

Huevos Rancheros

Ingredients:

- 2 corn tortillas
- 2 large eggs
- 1/2 cup salsa
- 1/4 cup refried beans
- 1/4 cup shredded cheese
- Fresh cilantro, for garnish
- Sour cream, for serving

Instructions:

1. Heat tortillas in a skillet.
2. Fry eggs sunny-side up.
3. Spread refried beans on tortillas, top with eggs, salsa, and cheese.
4. Garnish with cilantro and serve with sour cream.

Orange Marmalade Scones

Ingredients:

- 2 cups all-purpose flour
- 1/4 cup sugar
- 1 tbsp baking powder
- 1/2 tsp salt
- 1/2 cup cold butter, cubed
- 1/2 cup heavy cream
- 1/4 cup orange marmalade

Instructions:

1. Preheat oven to 375°F (190°C).
2. In a bowl, combine dry ingredients and cut in butter until mixture resembles crumbs.
3. Add cream and marmalade, stirring until dough forms.
4. Roll out dough, cut into wedges, and bake for 15-20 minutes.

Ricotta Pancakes with Mixed Berries

Ingredients:

- 1 cup ricotta cheese
- 1 cup all-purpose flour
- 1/2 cup milk
- 2 large eggs
- 2 tbsp sugar
- 1 tsp vanilla extract
- 1/2 cup mixed berries

Instructions:

1. In a bowl, whisk together ricotta, milk, eggs, sugar, and vanilla.
2. Add flour and mix until smooth.
3. Cook pancakes on a griddle, then top with fresh mixed berries.

Chia Seed Pudding with Mango

Ingredients:

- 1/4 cup chia seeds
- 1 cup coconut milk
- 1 tbsp maple syrup
- 1/2 ripe mango, diced

Instructions:

1. Combine chia seeds, coconut milk, and maple syrup.
2. Refrigerate for at least 4 hours, or overnight, until it thickens.
3. Top with fresh mango before serving.

Mushroom and Spinach Scramble

Ingredients:

- 2 cups mushrooms, sliced
- 1 cup spinach, chopped
- 4 large eggs
- 1 tbsp butter
- Salt and pepper, to taste
  Instructions:
1. Sauté mushrooms in butter until soft.
2. Add spinach and cook until wilted.
3. Scramble eggs into the mixture, season with salt and pepper, and cook until set.

Coconut Flour Waffles

Ingredients:

- 1/4 cup coconut flour
- 1/2 tsp baking powder
- 1/4 tsp salt
- 4 large eggs
- 1/2 cup milk
- 1 tsp vanilla extract
- 2 tbsp melted butter

Instructions:

1. Preheat waffle iron and grease lightly.
2. Whisk together coconut flour, baking powder, and salt.
3. In another bowl, combine eggs, milk, vanilla, and butter.
4. Mix dry and wet ingredients, then cook waffles until golden.

Quinoa Breakfast Bowl with Almonds

Ingredients:

- 1/2 cup cooked quinoa
- 1/2 cup almond milk
- 1 tbsp honey
- 1/4 cup sliced almonds
- Fresh fruit (berries or banana), for topping

Instructions:

1. Warm cooked quinoa in almond milk and honey.
2. Top with sliced almonds and fresh fruit before serving.

Sausage and Egg Muffins

Ingredients:

- 1 lb breakfast sausage
- 6 large eggs
- 1/2 cup shredded cheddar cheese
- 1/4 cup milk
- 1/2 tsp salt
- 1/4 tsp black pepper
- 1 tbsp olive oil
- 1/4 cup green onions, chopped

Instructions:

1. Preheat oven to 350°F (175°C) and grease a muffin tin.
2. Brown sausage in a skillet, then drain and set aside.
3. Whisk eggs, milk, cheese, salt, and pepper together.
4. Pour egg mixture into muffin tin, top with sausage, and bake for 15-18 minutes.

Apple Cranberry Oatmeal

Ingredients:

- 1 cup rolled oats
- 2 cups water or milk
- 1/2 apple, diced
- 1/4 cup dried cranberries
- 1 tbsp maple syrup
- 1/2 tsp cinnamon

Instructions:

1. Combine oats, water (or milk), and cinnamon in a pot.
2. Bring to a simmer, then cook until oats are tender.
3. Stir in apples, cranberries, and maple syrup. Serve warm.

Mediterranean Breakfast Wrap

Ingredients:

- 1 whole wheat tortilla
- 2 large eggs, scrambled
- 1/4 cup feta cheese
- 1/4 cup chopped tomatoes
- 1/4 cup cucumber, diced
- 1 tbsp olive tapenade (optional)
- Fresh parsley, for garnish
  Instructions:

1. Scramble eggs and season with salt and pepper.
2. Warm tortilla and layer with scrambled eggs, feta, tomatoes, cucumber, and tapenade.
3. Wrap up and garnish with parsley before serving.

Blueberry Lemon Muffins

Ingredients:

- 1 1/2 cups all-purpose flour
- 1/2 cup sugar
- 1 tsp baking powder
- 1/2 tsp baking soda
- 1/2 tsp salt
- 1/2 cup sour cream
- 1/4 cup melted butter
- 2 large eggs
- 1 cup fresh blueberries
- Zest of 1 lemon
- 1 tbsp lemon juice

Instructions:

1. Preheat oven to 375°F (190°C) and grease muffin tin.
2. Mix dry ingredients in one bowl and wet ingredients in another.
3. Combine wet and dry ingredients, then fold in blueberries and lemon zest.
4. Fill muffin tin and bake for 18-20 minutes.

Savory Breakfast Strata with Bacon

Ingredients:

- 6 slices of bread, cubed
- 4 large eggs
- 1 cup milk
- 1/2 cup cooked bacon, crumbled
- 1/2 cup shredded cheddar cheese
- 1/4 cup chopped green onions
- Salt and pepper, to taste

Instructions:

1. Preheat oven to 350°F (175°C).
2. Layer cubed bread in a greased baking dish.
3. Whisk eggs, milk, bacon, cheese, onions, salt, and pepper together, then pour over bread.
4. Bake for 30-35 minutes until set and golden.

Classic Eggs Benedict

Ingredients:

- 4 large eggs
- 2 English muffins, split and toasted
- 4 slices Canadian bacon
- 1/2 cup hollandaise sauce (store-bought or homemade)

Instructions:

1. Poach eggs by simmering water with a splash of vinegar and cooking eggs for 3-4 minutes.
2. Heat Canadian bacon in a skillet until warm.
3. Place bacon on toasted English muffin halves, top with poached eggs, and drizzle with hollandaise sauce.

Grilled Peach and Honey Yogurt Parfait

Ingredients:

- 2 peaches, halved and pitted
- 1 cup Greek yogurt
- 2 tbsp honey
- 1/4 cup granola
- Fresh mint leaves, for garnish

Instructions:

1. Grill peach halves until slightly charred, about 3-4 minutes per side.
2. In a glass, layer Greek yogurt, grilled peach slices, honey, and granola.
3. Garnish with fresh mint leaves and serve immediately.

Egg and Avocado Breakfast Sandwich

Ingredients:

- 2 slices whole grain bread
- 1 large egg
- 1/2 avocado, sliced
- 1 tbsp mayonnaise or aioli
- Salt and pepper, to taste
- 1 tbsp olive oil

Instructions:

1. Toast the bread slices.
2. Heat olive oil in a skillet and fry the egg to your preferred doneness.
3. Spread mayonnaise on the toasted bread.
4. Assemble the sandwich by layering avocado slices and the fried egg on one slice of bread. Season with salt and pepper, then top with the second slice of bread.

Sweet Corn and Bacon Fritters

Ingredients:

- 1 cup corn kernels (fresh or frozen)
- 4 slices bacon, cooked and crumbled
- 1/2 cup all-purpose flour
- 1/4 cup cornmeal
- 1 tsp baking powder
- 1/2 tsp salt
- 1/4 tsp black pepper
- 1/2 cup milk
- 1 large egg
- 2 tbsp chopped fresh chives
- Vegetable oil, for frying

Instructions:

1. In a bowl, combine flour, cornmeal, baking powder, salt, and pepper.
2. Whisk together milk and egg, then stir in corn kernels, bacon, and chives.
3. Heat oil in a skillet over medium heat.
4. Drop spoonfuls of the batter into the skillet and cook until golden brown on both sides, about 3-4 minutes per side.
5. Drain on paper towels and serve warm.

Baked Pears with Cinnamon and Walnuts

Ingredients:

- 4 pears, halved and cored
- 1/4 cup chopped walnuts
- 2 tbsp honey
- 1 tsp ground cinnamon
- 1/4 tsp ground nutmeg
- 1 tbsp butter

Instructions:

1. Preheat oven to 375°F (190°C).
2. Arrange pear halves in a baking dish.
3. Sprinkle with cinnamon, nutmeg, and walnuts.
4. Drizzle with honey and dot with butter.
5. Bake for 20-25 minutes, until pears are tender. Serve warm.

Sweet Potato and Sausage Casserole

Ingredients:

- 2 large sweet potatoes, peeled and diced
- 1 lb breakfast sausage, crumbled
- 1/2 onion, diced
- 1/2 cup shredded cheddar cheese
- 4 large eggs
- 1/2 tsp salt
- 1/4 tsp black pepper
- 1 tbsp olive oil

Instructions:

1. Preheat oven to 350°F (175°C).
2. Heat olive oil in a skillet and cook the sausage with onion until browned.
3. Meanwhile, cook the diced sweet potatoes in a separate skillet until tender, about 10-12 minutes.
4. In a greased casserole dish, layer the cooked sausage, sweet potatoes, and cheese.
5. Whisk eggs with salt and pepper, then pour over the casserole.
6. Bake for 25-30 minutes, until eggs are set and golden.

Maple-Glazed Oatmeal with Pecans

Ingredients:

- 1 cup rolled oats
- 2 cups water or milk
- 2 tbsp maple syrup
- 1/4 cup chopped pecans
- 1/2 tsp cinnamon
- Pinch of salt

Instructions:

1. In a saucepan, bring water (or milk) to a boil.
2. Stir in oats and salt, then reduce heat to low and cook until oats are tender, about 5 minutes.
3. Stir in maple syrup and cinnamon.
4. Top with chopped pecans and serve warm.

Spicy Shakshuka

Ingredients:

- 2 tbsp olive oil
- 1/2 onion, diced
- 1 bell pepper, diced
- 2 cloves garlic, minced
- 1 tsp ground cumin
- 1 tsp paprika
- 1/4 tsp cayenne pepper
- 1 can (14 oz) crushed tomatoes
- 4 large eggs
- Salt and pepper, to taste
- Fresh cilantro, for garnish

Instructions:

1. Heat olive oil in a large skillet and sauté onion, bell pepper, and garlic until soft.
2. Add cumin, paprika, and cayenne pepper, then stir in the crushed tomatoes.
3. Simmer the sauce for 10-15 minutes, seasoning with salt and pepper.
4. Make small wells in the sauce and crack eggs into the wells.
5. Cover and cook for 5-8 minutes, until the eggs are set.
6. Garnish with fresh cilantro and serve warm with crusty bread.

Cinnamon Apple Pancakes

Ingredients:

- 1 cup all-purpose flour
- 1 tbsp sugar
- 1 tsp baking powder
- 1/2 tsp ground cinnamon
- 1/4 tsp salt
- 1/2 cup milk
- 1 large egg
- 1 apple, peeled and finely chopped
- 2 tbsp butter, melted

Instructions:

1. In a bowl, whisk together flour, sugar, baking powder, cinnamon, and salt.
2. In another bowl, beat the milk, egg, and melted butter together.
3. Combine the wet and dry ingredients, then fold in the chopped apple.
4. Cook pancakes on a hot, greased griddle until golden brown on both sides. Serve warm.

Breakfast Salad with Poached Eggs

Ingredients:

- 4 cups mixed greens
- 1/2 avocado, sliced
- 1/2 cup cherry tomatoes, halved
- 1/4 red onion, thinly sliced
- 2 poached eggs
- 1 tbsp olive oil
- 1 tsp balsamic vinegar
- Salt and pepper, to taste

Instructions:

1. Arrange the mixed greens, avocado, tomatoes, and red onion on plates.
2. Drizzle with olive oil and balsamic vinegar, then season with salt and pepper.
3. Top each salad with a poached egg and serve immediately.

Chorizo Breakfast Bowl

Ingredients:

- 1/2 lb chorizo sausage, crumbled
- 2 large eggs
- 1/2 cup cooked rice or quinoa
- 1/4 cup shredded cheddar cheese
- 1/4 cup salsa
- 1/4 cup sour cream
- 1/4 avocado, sliced
- Fresh cilantro, for garnish
- Salt and pepper, to taste

Instructions:

1. In a skillet, cook chorizo over medium heat until browned and fully cooked.
2. In a separate pan, scramble the eggs and season with salt and pepper.
3. In a bowl, layer cooked rice or quinoa, chorizo, scrambled eggs, and cheese.
4. Top with salsa, sour cream, avocado slices, and fresh cilantro. Serve immediately.

Kiwi and Coconut Breakfast Pudding

Ingredients:

- 1/2 cup chia seeds
- 1 cup coconut milk
- 1 tbsp maple syrup
- 1/2 tsp vanilla extract
- 2 kiwis, peeled and diced

Instructions:

1. In a bowl, combine chia seeds, coconut milk, maple syrup, and vanilla extract. Stir well.
2. Refrigerate the mixture for at least 4 hours or overnight to thicken.
3. Before serving, top with fresh kiwi cubes. Serve chilled.

Avocado Toast with Tomato and Basil

Ingredients:

- 2 slices whole-grain bread, toasted
- 1 ripe avocado, mashed
- 1 small tomato, sliced
- Fresh basil leaves
- Salt and pepper, to taste
- Olive oil drizzle (optional)

Instructions:

1. Spread mashed avocado on the toasted bread.
2. Layer with tomato slices and fresh basil leaves.
3. Season with salt and pepper and drizzle with olive oil, if desired. Serve immediately.

Almond Joy Smoothie Bowl

Ingredients:

- 1 banana, frozen
- 1/2 cup almond milk
- 1/4 cup shredded coconut
- 2 tbsp almond butter
- 1 tbsp cocoa powder
- 1 tbsp honey
- 1/4 cup chopped almonds
- Chocolate chips, for topping (optional)

Instructions:

1. In a blender, combine banana, almond milk, coconut, almond butter, cocoa powder, and honey. Blend until smooth.
2. Pour the smoothie into a bowl and top with chopped almonds and chocolate chips. Serve immediately.

Egg and Spinach Breakfast Wrap

Ingredients:

- 2 large eggs
- 1/2 cup fresh spinach, chopped
- 1 whole-wheat tortilla
- 1/4 cup shredded cheese (optional)
- Salt and pepper, to taste
- 1 tbsp olive oil

Instructions:

1. In a skillet, heat olive oil and sauté spinach until wilted.
2. Beat the eggs, then add to the pan with spinach and scramble until fully cooked.
3. Place the egg and spinach mixture in the center of a whole-wheat tortilla and sprinkle with cheese (if using).
4. Fold the sides of the tortilla and roll it up into a wrap. Serve warm.

Chocolate Peanut Butter Overnight Oats

Ingredients:

- 1/2 cup rolled oats
- 1/2 cup milk (dairy or non-dairy)
- 1 tbsp peanut butter
- 1 tbsp cocoa powder
- 1 tbsp honey or maple syrup
- 1/4 tsp vanilla extract
- 1 tbsp chocolate chips (optional)

Instructions:

1. In a jar or bowl, combine oats, milk, peanut butter, cocoa powder, honey, and vanilla extract. Stir well.
2. Refrigerate overnight or for at least 4 hours to allow the oats to absorb the liquid.
3. Before serving, top with chocolate chips (if desired). Serve chilled.

Buttermilk Biscuits with Sausage Gravy

Ingredients:

- **For the biscuits**:
    - 2 cups all-purpose flour
    - 1 tbsp baking powder
    - 1/2 tsp salt
    - 1/2 cup unsalted butter, cold and cubed
    - 3/4 cup buttermilk
- **For the sausage gravy**:
    - 1 lb breakfast sausage
    - 2 tbsp all-purpose flour
    - 2 cups milk
    - Salt and pepper, to taste
    - **Instructions**:

1. **Make the biscuits**: Preheat oven to 425°F (220°C). In a large bowl, mix flour, baking powder, and salt. Cut in cold butter until the mixture resembles coarse crumbs. Stir in buttermilk until just combined. Turn dough onto a floured surface and pat it into a 1-inch thick rectangle. Cut into rounds and place on a baking sheet. Bake for 12-15 minutes, until golden brown.
2. **Make the gravy**: In a skillet, cook sausage over medium heat until browned, breaking it up as it cooks. Sprinkle the sausage with flour and stir to coat. Gradually add milk, stirring constantly, and cook until thickened. Season with salt and pepper.
3. Serve the biscuits with a generous spoonful of sausage gravy.

Mango Coconut Pancakes

Ingredients:

- 1 cup all-purpose flour
- 1 tbsp sugar
- 1 tsp baking powder
- 1/2 tsp baking soda
- 1/4 tsp salt
- 1/2 cup coconut milk
- 1/2 cup milk
- 1 large egg
- 1/2 tsp vanilla extract
- 1/2 cup diced mango
- 1/4 cup shredded coconut

Instructions:

1. In a large bowl, whisk together flour, sugar, baking powder, baking soda, and salt. In another bowl, combine coconut milk, milk, egg, and vanilla extract.
2. Pour the wet ingredients into the dry ingredients and stir until just combined. Gently fold in the diced mango and shredded coconut.
3. Heat a griddle or skillet over medium heat and lightly grease with butter or oil. Pour 1/4 cup of batter onto the griddle and cook until bubbles form on the surface. Flip and cook for an additional 1-2 minutes.
4. Serve the pancakes warm, topped with extra mango and coconut, if desired.

Bacon and Egg Breakfast Pizza

Ingredients:

- 1 pizza dough (store-bought or homemade)
- 1 tbsp olive oil
- 4 slices bacon, cooked and crumbled
- 2 large eggs
- 1/2 cup shredded mozzarella cheese
- 1/4 cup grated Parmesan cheese
- Salt and pepper, to taste
- Fresh basil, for garnish

Instructions:

1. Preheat oven to 475°F (245°C). Roll out the pizza dough on a floured surface to your desired thickness. Place on a baking sheet and brush with olive oil.
2. Sprinkle the mozzarella and Parmesan cheese over the dough. Make two small wells in the cheese for the eggs.
3. Crack the eggs into the wells, sprinkle with bacon, and season with salt and pepper.
4. Bake for 10-12 minutes, or until the egg whites are set but yolks are still soft.
5. Remove from oven and garnish with fresh basil. Slice and serve immediately.

Yogurt Parfait with Berries and Almonds

Ingredients:

- 1 cup Greek yogurt
- 1/2 cup mixed berries (strawberries, blueberries, raspberries)
- 2 tbsp sliced almonds
- 1 tbsp honey or maple syrup
- 1/4 tsp vanilla extract

Instructions:

1. In a small bowl, combine Greek yogurt, honey, and vanilla extract. Stir until smooth.
2. In serving glasses, layer the yogurt mixture with mixed berries and sliced almonds.
3. Repeat the layers and top with additional berries and almonds.
4. Serve immediately, or refrigerate for up to 2 hours.

Grilled Cheese Breakfast Sandwich

Ingredients:

- 2 slices of bread
- 2 slices cheddar cheese
- 1 egg
- 1 tbsp butter
- Salt and pepper, to taste
- Fresh herbs, for garnish (optional)

Instructions:

1. Heat a non-stick skillet over medium heat and melt the butter.
2. Place one slice of bread in the skillet and top with a slice of cheese. Cook until the bread is golden brown, then flip the sandwich over.
3. Crack the egg into the skillet and cook to your desired doneness. Season with salt and pepper.
4. Once the egg is cooked, assemble the sandwich by placing the egg on top of the melted cheese. Top with the second slice of bread and press down lightly.
5. Serve immediately, garnished with fresh herbs if desired.

www.ingramcontent.com/pod-product-compliance
Lightning Source LLC
LaVergne TN
LVHW081502060526
838201LV00056BA/2887